IMMIGRANTS
WHO BUILT AN EMPIRE

BY JESSICA GUNDERSON

CAPSTONE PRESS
a capstone imprint

Capstone Captivate is published by Capstone Press, an imprint of Capstone.
1710 Roe Crest Drive
North Mankato, Minnesota 56003
www.capstonepub.com

Library of Congress Cataloging-in-Publication Data is available
on the Library of Congress website.

ISBN: 978-1-4966-9595-6 (library binding)
ISBN: 978-1-4966-9679-3 (paperback)
ISBN: 978-1-9771-5442-2 (ebook pdf)

Summary: Some of the most important American industries and ideas stem from
people born outside the United States. Immigrants have had a major influence on
daily life in the United States, from how Americans search the internet and use
their phones to the clothes they wear and the buildings in which they live. Meet 25+
immigrants who built empires as artists, scientists, writers, musicians, inventors, and
entrepreneurs.

Image Credits

Associated Press: Gregorio Marrero, 38; Courtesy of Reetu Gupta: 5 (top right), 18;
Getty Images: Archive Photos/Hackett, 45, The Washington Post/Deb Lindsey, 58;
Library of Congress: 5 (middle right, bottom left), 21, 33, 36; Newscom: MAXPPP/
Christian Vioujard, 42, Photoshot/WEF, 51, Reuters/Aly Song, 23, Reuters/Brendan
McDermid, 30, Reuters/Lucas Jackson, 55, SIPA/FOX, 7, TNS/Bay Area News
Group/Aric Crabb, 53, Xinhua News Agency/Li Muzi, 40, ZUMA Press/Globe
Photos/Clinton Wallace, 9, ZUMA Press/Mark Richards, 14, 25, ZUMA Press/
Martin Klimek, 10; Shutterstock: a katz, 57, Albert H. Teich, 5 (bottom right), 35,
catwalker, 5 (top left), 16, dibrova, cover, 1, 5 (background), Everett Collection, 46,
GiuseppeCrimeni, 27, Huang Zheng, 43, My Hardy (background texture), 11, 27, 57,
TungCheung, 49, Uladzik Kryhin, 11; Sincerely Nellie Photography: 5 (middle left),
28; Svetlana Zhurkin: 12

Editorial Credits

Editor: Michelle Bisson; Designers: Kayla Rossow and Tracy Davies;
Media Researcher: Svetlana Zhurkin; Production Specialist: Tori Abraham

All internet sites appearing in back matter were available and accurate when this
book was sent to press.

TABLE OF CONTENTS

INTRODUCTION

"Give me your tired, your poor, your huddled masses yearning to breathe free." These words engraved on the Statue of Liberty in New York Harbor reflect the importance of immigration in our nation's history.

For centuries, immigration has been an essential building block of the United States. Immigrants cross oceans and borders in search of a new life. With them, they bring innovations, inventions, and ideas. They are entrepreneurs, designers, computer whizzes, and scientists. Their bold and brave business ventures have helped make the nation strong and prosperous.

Reetu Gupta

Jan Koum

Andrew Carnegie

Mina Yoo

Joseph Pulitzer

Arianna Huffington

5

CHAPTER ONE

IMMIGRANTS IN THE INTERNET WORLD

From Google to WhatsApp, immigrants have made their mark on the internet. Some invented search engines. Others created apps and social media sites. Immigrants' innovations on the internet have changed the nation and, in turn, the world.

SERGEY BRIN

(1973–)
Born in Moscow, Russia

In a small apartment in Moscow, Russia, Mikhail Brin made an announcement to his family. He told them they could no longer stay there. Four-year-old Sergey Brin was too young to understand what his father meant, but he knew it was important.

The year was 1977. Russia was part of the Soviet Union and under communist rule. Mikhail Brin wanted different opportunities for his family. In 1979, the Brins moved to Maryland.

Sergey Brin (right) and his friend Larry Page forever changed the way we search the internet when they created Google.

In 1995, Sergey Brin enrolled in graduate school at Stanford University in California. There, Brin became friends with Larry Page. The two began a joint research project involving information on the internet. In 1996, Page had the idea to rank a website based on how many other sites link to that site. The pair realized they could use the ranking method to create a search engine. In Page's dorm room, they tested their new search engine method. They named it Google.

At first, no one was interested in their search engine. Brin and Page decided to launch it themselves. They dropped out of Stanford, scraped together enough money to buy some servers, and rented a garage in Menlo Park, California. Their efforts soon gained attention. The cofounder of Sun Microsystems invested $100,000 to get them started.

Google quickly grew. The company is now worth hundreds of billions of dollars. And it all started with an immigrant and his friend in a dorm room.

STEVE CHEN

(1978–)
Born in Taipei, Taiwan

On Valentine's Day 2005 some friends took videos of a dinner party they attended. They realized there was no easy way to share the videos online with others. So they created a video-sharing website. Users could upload a video to the site, and the video would play in a web browser. By the end of the night, the friends named their website: YouTube.

One of those friends was Steve Chen. When he was 8, the Chen family immigrated to the United States. Chen didn't know any English. He spoke only

Mandarin, a form of Chinese. But he picked up English quickly at his new Chicago school.

In 1999, Chen was offered a job at PayPal, a service that helps people buy and sell things securely online. He jumped at the chance and moved to California. At PayPal he met Chad Hurley and Jawed Karim.

After cocreating YouTube, Steve Chen went on to cofound the company AVOS Systems, Inc., build a video-sharing app called MixBit, and work with Google Ventures.

After the 2005 dinner party, the three friends worked to make YouTube a reality. In May, the site became available for public use in its testing form. The site grew in popularity over the next several months. In October 2006, Google bought YouTube for $1.65 billion.

Chen has been named one of *Business 2.0* magazine's "50 Most Influential People."

JAWED KARIM

(1979–)
Born in Merseburg, East Germany

Jawed Karim was born in communist East Germany. His mother was German and his father was Bangladeshi. The young family faced much prejudice because of their mixed heritage. They wondered if West Germany would be friendlier. In the early 1980s, the Karims moved there.

When Karim was 13, his family immigrated to St. Paul, Minnesota. Karim studied computer science at the University of Illinois at Champaign-Urbana. But he left college to take a job at PayPal in California, where he met Steve Chen and Chad Hurley.

In 2005, the three friends created YouTube, a video-sharing website. Karim uploaded the first

Jawed Karim (right) and his friends Chad Hurley (left) and Steve Chen made millions when they sold YouTube to Google in 2006.

video, and YouTube went live. Titled *Me at the Zoo*, the video shows Karim visiting the San Diego Zoo.

Early on, Karim decided not to take part in the daily business of YouTube. He wanted to be a student. While Chen and Hurley became the public face of YouTube, Karim focused on his studies at Stanford University. When Google bought YouTube in 2006, Karim received $64 million in stock.

SILICON VALLEY

Silicon Valley, a region near San Francisco, California, is known as the center of technology and social media. In the mid-20th century, the area became popular for electronics research and computer manufacturing. The

Apple's ring-shaped campus is just one of many high-tech headquarters in Silicon Valley.

region was named "Silicon Valley" after silicon, a chemical element used as a conductor in computer circuitry. The area also hosts a large number of start-up companies.

Thousands of high-tech firms are headquartered in Silicon Valley. Among them are Tesla, PayPal, Apple, Facebook, Intel, Twitter, and Hewlett-Packard. Silicon Valley offers many business opportunities for those interested in computer technology.

IKA ALIYEVA

(1981–)
Born in Lankaran, Azerbaijan

In southern Azerbaijan, where Ika Aliyeva grew up, women were not accepted as leaders. But Aliyeva strove to break that mold.

Aliyeva's parents encouraged their daughter to be powerful and strong-minded. When Aliyeva was 30 years old, she moved to the United States to study marketing and social media. A few years later, she and her husband moved to San Francisco.

By 2020, Ika Aliyeva's Femigrants online community topped 10,000 members.

The couple struggled to make ends meet. Aliyeva found it difficult to find a good job. As an immigrant, she felt as though she didn't belong in any workplace. Eventually, she found a job, but she never forgot her struggles finding work. She wanted to help other female immigrants achieve their dreams and become business leaders. In 2017, she created an online community for immigrant women. She called it Femigrants. Her goal was to create a place where women from different races, cultures, and ethnic backgrounds could support each other.

Femigrants began with about 25 members. Within a year, membership grew to 3,000 nationwide. Femigrants offers mentorship opportunities, events, and workshops to help its members become business leaders and entrepreneurs.

JERRY YANG

(1968–)
Born in Taipei, Taiwan

The only English word Jerry Yang knew when he arrived in California in 1978 was "shoe." He was 10 years old. He became fluent in English in three years.

Jerry Yang is considered an internet pioneer for his work cocreating Yahoo! with David Filo in the 1990s.

He served as student body president and graduated at the top of his high school class.

Yang attended Stanford University as an undergraduate. He stayed there to earn his doctoral degree. In 1994, he and his friend David Filo began making lists of their favorite websites. They created a website called "Jerry and David's Guide to the World Wide Web." The website was a directory of other sites, organized in a hierarchy. In March 1994, they renamed the website Yahoo!

By the end of 1994, the website had received more than 1 million hits. In March 1995, Yang and Filo incorporated Yahoo!, or made it into a company. The company received about $2 million in investments. Yang was Yahoo!'s CEO, or leader, from 2007 to 2009. He continued serving on Yahoo!'s board until 2012.

After stepping away from Yahoo!, Yang founded AME Cloud Ventures, which funds start-up companies. In 2017, he gave $25 million to the Asian Art Museum of San Francisco.

JAN KOUM

(1976–)
Born in Fastiv, Ukraine

When Jan Koum was growing up in a small village in communist Ukraine, which was then part of the Soviet Union, his parents rarely talked to anyone on the phone. They knew the government had bugged their phone lines. Koum grew up without any sense of privacy.

In 1992, when Koum was 16, he, his mother, and his grandmother immigrated to Mountain View, California.

Jan Koum speaks about WhatsApp at the 2014 Mobile World Congress in Barcelona, Spain.

Koum got a job cleaning a grocery store to make ends meet. He taught himself computer programming and landed a job at Yahoo!

After nine years at Yahoo!, Koum quit his job to travel. In January 2009, he bought an iPhone. As he was looking at the newly introduced App Store, he realized the app business was a growing field. He'd been thinking about ways people could message friends around the world without having to pay international texting fees. An app might be able to do just that.

Koum chose the name "WhatsApp" because it sounded like "what's up." Remembering his childhood in communist Ukraine, he wanted the app to only store phone numbers. No personal information would be kept. Along with partner Brian Acton, Koum made his idea a reality.

By 2011, WhatsApp ranked in the top 20 of all U.S. apps. In 2014, Koum sold WhatsApp to Facebook for $19 billion.

Koum wanted to sign the deal with Facebook in a significant place. He chose an old, white building where he once stood in line for food stamps. His was a true rags-to-riches story.

DID YOU KNOW?

In 2018, 44 percent of Fortune 500 companies—U.S. companies with the highest revenue—had been founded by first- or second-generation immigrants.

REETU GUPTA

(1972–)
Born in Kaithal, India

Reetu Gupta received a Female Entrepreneur of the Year award for her work on Cirkled In and wants her legacy to be the enhancement of education systems.

When Reetu Gupta was 8 years old, she began knocking on doors in her small town in India. Her goal was to convince families to send their kids to her mother's school. Nearly 70 percent of residents in Gupta's small town couldn't read. Gupta and her mother, a teacher, hoped to change that.

Gupta's childhood experiences taught her the importance of education. After receiving an engineering degree along with a masters in engineering, she moved to Washington State to work for AT&T Wireless. In 2010, she earned an MBA from the University of Washington.

When her daughter was applying to a private middle school, Gupta helped with her application. Gupta noticed how hard it was to track down her daughter's academic and extracurricular achievements. She realized the need to help students organize their accomplishments.

In 2015, Gupta created an online platform called Cirkled In. There, students can create portfolios in a secure manner and can share them with any application from colleges and scholarships to jobs and internships. By showcasing themselves in the best possible way, students increase success for all applications. Universities also use Cirkled In to seek out the best candidates for their programs.

By early 2020, Cirkled In had more than 350,000 student users. Gupta received national awards, including the Grand Award from the American Business Awards, given to the top 10 companies in the United States.

CHAPTER TWO

IMMIGRANTS IN TECHNOLOGY

As inventors and creators, immigrants have had an impact on the technology people use every day. The telephone was the idea of an immigrant from Scotland. Computer-chip maker Intel wouldn't be successful without the determination of a Hungarian immigrant. The electric car Tesla exists because of a South African immigrant. Immigrants' lasting influence on technology is far-reaching.

ALEXANDER GRAHAM BELL

(1847–1922)
Born in Edinburgh, Scotland

"Mr. Watson, come here. I want to see you," Alexander Graham Bell said. Those were the first words ever spoken over a telephone.

Bell grew up around the hearing-impaired. His mother had hearing loss, and his father taught Deaf students. Later, Bell would become a teacher

Long before
the internet,
Alexander
Graham Bell
brought the world
closer together
with his invention
of the telephone.

of the Deaf as well. His interests in sound and communication led him to create one of the world's most important inventions, the telephone.

Bell was born in 1847 in Edinburgh, Scotland. In 1870, he moved with his family to Ontario, Canada. One year later, Bell moved to Massachusetts, where he taught at the Boston School for Deaf Mutes.

Bell experimented with transmitting sound. He discovered how to send musical notes over the telegraph. This led him to discover how to transmit the human voice. In February 1876, he filed a patent for the telephone.

Bell's father-in-law helped him start Bell Telephone Company. In 1880, the French government awarded Bell the Volta Prize for electrical science. With the prize money, Bell set up the Volta Laboratory. The lab studied deafness and how to improve life for the Deaf.

Today, the Bell Telephone Company is known as AT&T. Bell's telephone is considered one of the most important inventions in history.

ELON MUSK

(1971–)
Born in Pretoria, South Africa

Elon Musk loved to play video games on his Atari. When he was 10 years old, he bought his own computer. He taught himself computer programming so he could create his own games. This sparked his passion for creating.

When Musk was 17, he moved to Ontario, Canada, for college. Two years later, he transferred to the University of Pennsylvania.

Musk has been a successful entrepreneur for decades. In 1995, he and his brother founded Global Link Information Network. In 1999, Compaq bought

Elon Musk speaks at an opening ceremony for Tesla's new Gigafactory in Shanghai, China, on January 7, 2020.

the business for $307 million in cash and $34 million in stock options. Musk then founded X.com, an online bank that eventually merged with PayPal.

Musk was always interested in space travel and rocket ships. His first idea was to send mice to Mars to see if they could survive. Then, he had the idea of sending a greenhouse to Mars. The greenhouse could create oxygen and perhaps make the planet a place for humans to live. He called this idea Mars Oasis. But the rockets he needed were too expensive to buy. He thought he could build them himself. In 2002, he founded Space Exploration Technologies, or SpaceX.

The company focuses on advancing rocket technology and manufacturing space launch vehicles. In 2020, SpaceX launched the first private flight to dock at the International Space Station.

In 2004, Musk joined the board of Tesla Motors, an electric vehicle company. Musk's goal was to make electric cars affordable in order to combat global warming. In 2006, he helped found SolarCity, a solar energy company.

In all his ventures, Musk continues to find ways for technology to benefit people and preserve the planet. In 2012, he signed the Giving Pledge, promising to give the majority of his wealth to charitable causes.

ANDY GROVE

(1936–2016)
Born in Budapest, Hungary

In 1944, when András Gróf was 7 years old, the Nazis invaded Hungary. They deported more than 500,000 Jewish people, including Gróf's father, to concentration camps. Gróf and his mother hid their Jewish identity. Gróf's father managed to survive the camps. He returned home after the war.

Andy Grove won many awards during his lifetime, including *Time* magazine's Man of the Year award in 1997.

In 1956, Hungarians rebelled against their communist government. Many of Gróf's friends were arrested. He decided to move to the United States. Gróf snuck across the border into Austria and boarded a refugee ship bound for New York City. He moved in with an aunt and uncle and changed his name to Andrew (Andy) Grove.

In the early 1960s, Grove worked for a computer science company. He and his team led research into using silicon to place transistors in computers. In 1968, he joined Intel Corporation the day it was founded.

Intel introduced the world's first microprocessor in 1971. In 1978, Intel unveiled the microchip. By 1997, Intel controlled 85 percent of the microchip market. The company's sales rose from $2,672 in 1971 to $20.8 billion in 1997.

Intel's success is largely credited to Grove. He was the company's president in 1979, its CEO in 1987, and its chairman in 1997. His management style was tough, but he encouraged brainstorming. Employees of any rank could propose ideas, as long as they could defend them.

Throughout life, Grove never forgot where he came from. He was a strong supporter of the International Rescue Committee, which helps refugees. He once said that "immigrants and immigration are what made America what it is. We must ... have a tolerance for differences, a tolerance for new people."

DID YOU KNOW?

Computer manufacturer IBM chose the Intel microchip for use in its first personal computer.

JEWISH PERSECUTION

European Jewish people are an ethnic and religious group that has long been oppressed. In Europe, over the centuries, many Jewish people faced persecution, and even death, because of their ethnicity and religion. In

Photographs at the United States Holocaust Memorial Museum in Washington, D.C., honor the millions of Jewish people who were persecuted by the Nazis during World War II.

many countries, Jewish people were forced to live in specific areas and were stripped of certain rights.

In Russia, anti-Jewish riots known as pogroms sparked fear and death in Jewish settlements. A wave of Russian pogroms from 1903 to 1906 killed nearly 2,500 Jewish people.

During World War II (1939–1945), the Nazi regime sent millions of European Jewish people to concentration camps. Approximately 6 million Jewish people were killed there. This genocide is known as the Holocaust.

Between 1938 and 1941, about 123,000 Jewish people immigrated to the U.S. to escape persecution. Many hundreds of thousands more applied but were denied. Once the U.S. entered the war, immigration was cut off. As of 2019, the Jewish American population stood at 7.5 million.

MINA YOO

(1974–)
Born in Seoul, South Korea

After Mina Yoo had her first baby, she decided to climb Mount Rainier. When training for the climb, she had to carry a lot of things with her, such as water, food, and a backpack. Having a new baby meant she carried a lot of items daily too, such as a diaper bag. When she needed her hands free or to take a rest,

Mina Yoo has sold more than 600,000 Heroclips around the world and expects revenue from her invention to pass the $1 million mark in 2020.

she realized there was no place to put her bag but on the ground. She wondered why no one had invented portable hooks on which to hang items. So, in 2015, she invented them herself.

Yoo was born in Seoul, South Korea. In 1991, she immigrated to the United States. She holds two PhDs, one in sociology and the other in business administration.

Yoo's invention, called Heroclip, is part hook and part carabiner. In 2016, she presented her invention at the GeekWire Summit meeting. Enthusiasm for Heroclip grew. Heroclip received $500,000 in funding in May 2017. More than 7,000 people funded the clip through Kickstarter and Indiegogo, which are crowdfunding sites.

Yoo used the money to make clips of different sizes and styles. Heroclip became popular throughout the world and can be found in hardware stores and online.

Through her Heroclip experience, Yoo realized how few inventors were women. In 2019, she coauthored a book titled *Be an InventHer: An Everywoman's Guide to Creating the Next Big Thing.*

AYAH BDEIR

(1982–)
Born in Montreal, Canada

Ayah Bdeir was born in Montreal, Canada, but grew up mostly in Beirut, Lebanon. Her parents taught her and her sisters to love math and science. As a child, Bdeir would often take things apart to see what was inside. She came to the United States at age 24 when war between Lebanon and Israel forced her to flee the country.

Ayah Bdeir poses with her staff at the littleBits corporate headquarters in New York City in 2014.

In 2011, Bdeir founded and ran a makerspace in New York City. A makerspace is a place for learning, exploring, inventing, and idea-sharing that uses tools. The equipment can include high-tech items like 3D printers, low-tech devices like sewing machines, or no-tech materials such as cardboard and art supplies. In her makerspace, Bdeir began experimenting with click-together electrical parts. She realized others could benefit from "playing" with the electrical pieces. She wanted to make electronics available to everyone.

Bdeir created littleBits later that year. LittleBits are domino-sized electrical units that snap together magnetically. Bdeir wanted her product to be useful in many ways. Teachers can use littleBits to teach electrical circuits. Inventors can use them to experiment with new inventions. Artists can use them to create designs. LittleBits raised $15.6 million to fuel its growth.

In 2014, *Inc.* magazine included Bdeir on its list of the "35 Under 35 Coolest Entrepreneurs." Four years later, the magazine named her as one of the "Top 5 Women to Watch in Robotics."

CHAPTER THREE

IMMIGRANTS WHO INFLUENCED THE ARTS

Excelling in writing, sports, and visual arts, immigrants have become icons in their fields. With good business sense, these immigrants have turned their talents into profit. Others have contributed money to the arts.

JOSEPH PULITZER

(1847–1911)
Born in Makó, Hungary

Joseph Pulitzer was a newspaper publisher. Today, his name is best known for the Pulitzer Prizes. The Pulitzer Prizes are given for achievements in journalism, literature, history, and music.

Joseph Pulitzer was born in 1847. After his father died in 1858, the family fell into poverty. To help make ends meet, Joseph enlisted in the army.

In 1864, the United States was embroiled in the Civil War (1861–1865). Recruiters from the

Union Army began paying European soldiers to enlist. Pulitzer immigrated to Boston at age 17. He served in the Union Army for eight months until the war ended. After the war, Pulitzer moved to St. Louis, Missouri.

By age 40, the time of this photo, Joseph Pulitzer was well on his way to becoming the world's most famous newspaper publisher.

In 1868, Pulitzer became a reporter for the *Westliche Post*, a German-language newspaper. In 1878, he bought two St. Louis newspapers, the *St. Louis Post* and the *St. Louis Dispatch*. He merged the two newspapers into one, the *St. Louis Post-Dispatch*. The new newspaper focused on exposing corruption, fraud, and crime. It soon became successful.

In 1883, Pulitzer bought a struggling newspaper, *New York World*. To increase readers' interests, Pulitzer began publishing sensational stories on crime, disaster, and scandal. *New York World*'s subscriptions grew from 15,000 to 600,000. It became the most popular newspaper in the country.

When Pulitzer died in 1911, he left Columbia University $2 million. The university set up the Graduate School of Journalism. In 1917, the graduate school awarded the first Pulitzer Prizes.

ARIANNA HUFFINGTON

(1950–)
Born in Athens, Greece

Arianna Huffington was born Ariadne-Anna Stassinopoulos in 1950. When she was 16, she moved to England to study at Cambridge University. She became president of the debate club, the first immigrant female to hold that title. She earned a master's degree in economics. In 1974, she published her first book, *The Female Woman*, a critique of the women's rights movement.

In 1980, Stassinopoulos moved to New York City. She later moved to California with her husband, Michael Huffington. He ran for the U.S. Senate in 1996. She was active in her husband's campaign. Although he lost, the campaign made her famous. The couple divorced in 1997, but Huffington continued to be politically active. She appeared on TV and radio, voicing her conservative opinions.

Arianna Huffington speaks at a National Press Club luncheon in Washington, D.C., in 2011.

In the early 2000s, Huffington began shifting her political views. She supported environmental causes and became antiwar. In 2005, she started *The Huffington Post*, a liberal-leaning website.

Over the next few years, *The Huffington Post* grew in popularity. In 2008, it was named the most powerful political blog in the world by the *Observer*. *Forbes* magazine named Huffington one of the most influential women in media in 2009. In 2011, Huffington sold *The Huffington Post* to AOL for more than $300 million.

ANDREW CARNEGIE

(1835–1919)
Born in Dunfermline, Scotland

As a boy in Scotland, Andrew Carnegie spent a lot of time at the library. Once grown, he never forgot his love for libraries. After he made his fortune, he helped create almost 3,000 public libraries.

Andrew Carnegie channeled his business success into improving literacy and education by funding thousands of libraries and colleges across the United States.

In 1848, Carnegie's family immigrated to Pennsylvania. At age 18, Carnegie began working in the telegraph office of the Pennsylvania Railroad Company. By the time he was 24, he had become a manager of the Western Division of the railroad. In 1865, he left the railroad and started Union Ironworks and Keystone Bridge Company.

Carnegie soon became interested in steel. He opened his first steel mill in 1875 and formed the Carnegie Steel Corporation. He bought out his competitor, Homestead Steel Works, in 1883. He combined the two into one company, Carnegie Steel Company. It was the largest steel company in the world.

In 1901, Carnegie retired. He sold Carnegie Steel to J.P. Morgan for $480 million.

Throughout his life, Carnegie donated much of his money. He gave to libraries and colleges. He started the Carnegie Institute (now Carnegie Mellon University) in Pittsburgh. By the end of his life, he'd given away $350 million. Libraries and museums bearing his name are peppered around the country and are lasting proof of this immigrant's generosity.

VALENTINA VITOLS BELLO

(c. 1974–)
Born in Caracas, Venezuela

Valentina Vitols Bello was born in Venezuela. She earned degrees in law and marketing before moving to the United States. There, she received a master's degree in photography from the Savannah College of Art and Design in Georgia. She opened her own photography business, called Valentina Vitols Studio, in Seattle, Washington. She photographs food, families, and nature. Her work has been featured on the Food Network and in many magazines.

Valentina Vitols Bello has used her success as a photographer to help other immigrant women start their own businesses.

Having a successful business made Bello want to help others. She understood how hard it was for immigrant women to open their own businesses and raise funding. She belongs to the investment firm Pipeline Angels. It finds funding for female and nonbinary entrepreneurs. She is also part of the Alliance of Angels. It funds start-up companies.

DIKEMBE MUTOMBO

(1966–)
Born in Kinshasa, Democratic Republic of the Congo

Dikembe Mutombo arrived in the United States with dreams of becoming a doctor. Instead, he found a career shooting hoops.

When he was a senior in high school in Kinshasa, Mutombo won an international science competition. He then received a scholarship to Georgetown University in Washington, D.C. He enrolled in 1987 as a premed student. Then, the Georgetown Hoyas basketball coach heard about the 7-foot-2 (218-centimeter) student from the Congo. The coach asked Mutombo to play, he agreed, and a basketball star was born.

Dikembe Mutombo takes part in a "Crime Prevention and Sustainable Development Through Sports" event at the United Nations headquarters in New York City in 2018.

Mutombo graduated from Georgetown in 1991. That year, the Denver Nuggets of the National Basketball Association (NBA) drafted him. He became one of the league's best defensive players. Mutombo went on to play for several other NBA teams and won four Defensive Player of the Year titles.

Mutombo supported his family back home in the Congo. In 1997, his mother had a stroke and died for lack of medical care. Mutombo made it his mission to aid the health of his home country. He started the Dikembe Mutombo Foundation to improve living conditions in the Congo.

One of Mutombo's major projects was to build a hospital in Kinshasa. The $29 million hospital opened in 2007. Mutombo named it the Biamba Marie Mutombo Hospital, after his mother.

Although Mutombo didn't become a doctor, he has helped save many lives.

IEOH MING PEI

(1917–2019)
Born in Guangzhou, China

Nine-year-old Ieoh Ming Pei watched in fascination as a 25-story hotel was constructed in Shanghai. He returned day after day to the spot. That's when he knew he wanted to design buildings.

Pei was born in 1917 in Guangzhou, China. He grew up in Hong Kong and Shanghai. At 17, Pei moved to the United States to study architecture.

Ieoh Ming Pei often combined simple geometric patterns, such as triangles, squares, and circles, with traditional architectural elements in his building designs.

In 1948, he became the architectural director of the firm Webb and Knapp. He designed projects such as the Mile High Center in Denver, Colorado, and the Hyde Park Redevelopment in Chicago, Illinois.

In 1955, Pei founded his own architectural firm, I.M. Pei & Associates. He designed many buildings around the world. One of his first major projects was the National Center for Atmospheric Research in Boulder, Colorado. It was completed in 1966. Its design was inspired by the American Indian cliff dwellings of southwest Colorado.

Pei also designed the East Building of the National Gallery of Art in Washington, D.C., and the Rock & Roll Hall of Fame in Cleveland, Ohio. One of his most famous designs is the Louvre Pyramid at the Louvre Museum in Paris, France.

Pei won several awards, including the Pritzker Prize and the Presidential Medal of Freedom. He used the $100,000 award from the Pritzker Prize to create a scholarship fund for Chinese architecture students.

Pei's Louvre Pyramid is made with 603 rhombus-shaped and 70 triangular pieces of glass. It houses an underground lobby for visitors entering the Louvre Museum in Paris, France.

CHAPTER FOUR

IMMIGRANTS IN FASHION

Models stride down the runway. Miners pan for gold. Young people go out with friends. All are dressed in designs brought to them by immigrants who made a lasting mark on the fashion world.

LEVI STRAUSS

(1829–1902)
Born in Buttenheim, Germany

Levi's jeans occupy racks, closets, and shelves around the world. They bear the name of the immigrant who first sold them, Levi Strauss.

Strauss was born to a Jewish family in Germany. In 1846, after his father died, Strauss joined two older brothers in New York. They owned a dry goods store, and Strauss worked for them.

In 1849, the California Gold Rush struck. Thousands of people raced to California to pan for gold. Miners and settlers needed clothing and goods. In 1853, Strauss opened a store in San Francisco. It was called Levi Strauss & Co. He sold goods such as clothing and bedding.

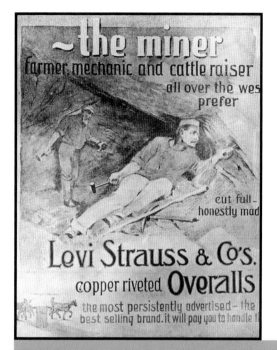

An advertisement from 1875 showcases Levi Strauss's riveted overalls, which were popular with miners at that time.

Levi Strauss & Co. was successful. But Strauss's claim to fame lay ahead. In 1872, Jacob Davis wrote to Strauss about a business idea. Davis had been buying denim cloth from Strauss and making sturdy pants with rivets on the seams. The rivets helped make the pants stronger. Davis wanted Strauss to sell the design in his store.

Within a year, they'd made $40,000 selling the pants. Soon, Strauss bought factory space to make them. The original design became the famous 501® jeans in 1890.

Strauss was generous with his earnings. He donated to a Jewish orphanage and helped establish the first synagogue in San Francisco. When he died in 1902, he left the company to his nephews. In 2019, the company's revenue was $5.8 billion. Levi's jeans remain part of American culture.

OSCAR DE LA RENTA

(1932–2014)
Born in Santo Domingo, Dominican Republic

Oscar de la Renta was born in the Dominican Republic. At 18, he went to Madrid, Spain, to study art. But he needed to make some extra money, so he

Oscar de la Renta shows off his Hall of Fame award at the Fragrance Foundation's 32nd Annual "FiFi" Awards in 2004.

began drawing clothes for fashion magazines and newspapers. In 1956, his designs caught the eye of the wife of the U.S. ambassador to Spain. She asked de la Renta to design a gown for her daughter. He accepted, never dreaming it would be featured on the cover of *Life* magazine.

After his gown appeared on *Life* magazine's cover, de la Renta worked for designers in Spain and Paris, France. He moved to New York City in 1963. There, he started his own fashion company.

De la Renta's designs often used ruffles and vibrant colors. He said his bright color palette was inspired by his childhood in the Caribbean. These designs became widely popular. Celebrities and first ladies from Jacqueline Kennedy to Michelle Obama wore his designs.

De la Renta didn't stop at clothing design. He launched his own fragrances, furniture, bridal wear, and accessories. In 2006, he also launched a line of less expensive clothing.

Although de la Renta became a U.S. citizen, he never forgot his Dominican roots. He contributed to the construction of a much-needed school there.

DO WON CHANG AND JIN SOOK CHANG

(1954– and 1963–)
Born in South Korea

In 1981, Do Won Chang and his wife, Jin Sook Chang, left Seoul, South Korea, for the United States. In 1984, the couple used the $11,000 they had in savings to open their first store, Fashion 21, in the Highland Park neighborhood of Los Angeles. The neighborhood was largely Korean American. The Changs marketed women's clothing to the Korean American community. They sold designs similar to those made in South Korea. They kept their prices affordable. Within the first year, the business made $700,000. The couple knew it was time to expand. They renamed the business Forever 21 and opened a second store.

Forever 21, with its hip, affordable clothing, became popular. The Changs began opening stores every six months. They expanded to include men's and children's clothing. By 2013, Forever 21 had 480 stores worldwide. They even opened one in the neighborhood of Seoul where Do Won grew up. The year 2015 saw the brand's biggest sales, at $4.4 billion.

In 2020, the Changs sold Forever 21 for $81 million. Their success, as Do Won once said, is the true American dream.

The Changs mixed trendy fashions with affordable prices to build Forever 21 into a worldwide retail empire.

CHAPTER FIVE

IMMIGRANTS IN FOOD

Throughout the centuries, immigrants have brought recipes from their homelands to the United States to share with others. From starting their own restaurants to leading companies, these immigrants have brought to the country an essential life staple—food.

INDRA NOOYI

(1955–)
Born in Chennai, India

Cricket player, all-girl rock band guitarist, CEO of a Fortune 500 Company—Indra Nooyi has done it all.

Nooyi grew up in a middle-class family and attended a private Catholic high school. In 1978, she moved to the United States. She was a manager at several companies first. Then she was hired by PepsiCo in 1994. She became vice president of corporate strategy and development.

Indra Nooyi speaks at the World Economic Forum in Davos, Switzerland, in 2008.

Nooyi proved herself to be an insightful leader with a strong vision. She led PepsiCo to buy other brands, including Tropicana and Quaker Oats. In 2006, she became its CEO. She was the first female to head the company.

Nooyi helped PepsiCo evolve. As Americans began turning away from sugary soft drinks, sales plummeted. Nooyi set her vision on healthier products. She put PepsiCo's products into three categories. The "fun for you" category was high-calorie snacks. "Better for you" were diet sodas and lower-calorie snacks. "Good for you" contained healthy foods. Nooyi's vision helped keep sales up.

By 2016, less than 25 percent of PepsiCo's sales were from soda.

In late 2018, Nooyi stepped down as PepsiCo's CEO. During her 12 years in the job, the company's sales grew 80 percent. The credit for that goes mostly to Nooyi.

DID YOU KNOW?

In 2019, the number of female CEOs of Fortune 500 companies reached an all-time high of 33. The other 467 were male.

ANDREW LY

(c. 1955–)
Born in Vietnam

A small boat, crowded with 148 refugees, set off into the waves of the South China Sea in 1978. Those on it were leaving war-torn South Vietnam. Andrew Ly, along with his parents and five siblings, looked to the new life ahead. But then pirates swept toward the boat. They stole everything except the clothes on the refugees' backs.

Andrew Ly (right) inspects packages of madeleine cookies in his Hayward, California, production facility in 2015.

Still, the Lys sailed on. In four days, the refugees landed in Malaysia. The Lys spent the next year in a refugee camp. Then they made their way to San Francisco, California. There, as many as nine family members lived in a one-bedroom apartment. At night, Ly and his four brothers made Vietnamese-style doughnuts.

The Lys decided to sell their doughnuts. In 1984, the brothers pooled $40,000 in savings. They used it to buy a small shop and named it Sugar Bowl Bakery. Andrew Ly, the accountant, was at the helm.

The Lys began by selling their doughnuts in their shop and to Chinese restaurants. They branched out to neighborhood groceries. As demand grew, they opened five more neighborhood bakeries.

Sugar Bowl Bakery soon became one of the largest food production companies in the San Francisco Bay area. Ly, now CEO of Sugar Bowl Bakery, will never forget his beginnings. "We came here as boat people, so we don't take things for granted," he said. "Success is a journey, not a destination."

HAMDI ULUKAYA

(1972–)
Born in Ilic, Turkey

Hamdi Ulukaya's family owned a sheep, goat, and dairy farm along the Euphrates River near Ilic, Turkey. The Kurdish Muslim family sold cheese and yogurt.

Hamdi Ulukaya used his experience growing up on a dairy farm in Turkey to build Chobani into a leading yogurt company in the United States.

As a young man, Ulukaya moved to the United States to study English. In 1997, he moved to upstate New York. There, he worked on a farm. In 2005, Ulukaya heard about an 84-year-old yogurt factory that had recently closed. He toured the plant and bought it.

Ulukaya wanted to make a different kind of yogurt than Americans were used to. He produced the type of strained yogurt he'd grown up with, known as Greek yogurt. He named his product Chobani, Turkish for "shepherd." For the recipe, he used only natural ingredients.

In 2007, Ulukaya sent his first shipment to a store on Long Island. The store kept buying more. In 2009, Costco picked up the brand. Chobani doubled its sales every year through 2013. After that, sales continued to rise.

Ulukaya often employs refugees in his factories. In 2017, the U.S. banned travelers and refugees from several largely Muslim countries. Ulukaya wrote that "America has always been a symbol of hope, tolerance and diversity—and these are values we must work very hard to uphold."

BAN ON IMMIGRANTS

Beginning in 2017, President Donald Trump issued executive orders banning or limiting travel and immigration from certain countries. The "travel ban," as it became known, was put in place to combat terrorism. The eight countries on the original list were largely Muslim. As of 2020, the travel ban included 13 countries. Eritrea, Iran, Kyrgyzstan, Libya, Myanmar, Nigeria, North Korea, Somalia, Sudan, Syria, Tanzania, Venezuela, and Yemen are all affected by the travel ban. Seven of these countries are mostly Muslim.

Critics called the travel ban unconstitutional and anti-Muslim. The White House maintained that the ban was in place for national security.

Thousands of people gathered in New York City's Battery Park on January 29, 2017, to protest President Trump's immigration ban.

CRISTINA MARTINEZ

(c. 1970s–)
Born in Capulhuac, Mexico

Cristina Martinez has been making barbacoa—slow-cooked meat—since she was 6 years old. Barbacoa is one of the signature dishes of her home of Capulhuac, Mexico. Cooking barbacoa makes Martinez feel something magical. She shares that magic with others.

Cristina Martinez and her husband, Ben Miller, stand outside their South Philly Barbocoa restaurant in Philadelphia, Pennsylvania.

In 2009, Martinez started on a dangerous journey across the desert. Her destination was the United States. She wanted to make money to send her daughter to school.

After crossing the border, she made her way to Philadelphia. She began working as a pastry chef. But the restaurant discovered her undocumented status and fired her. Because of this, she was banned from gaining permanent legal U.S. resident status.

Martinez and her husband began selling barbacoa tacos out of a cart on weekends. The tacos were popular. In 2015, they opened a permanent location called South Philly Barbacoa. In 2019, Martinez was nominated for the prestigious James Beard Award for Best Chef.

Martinez is still without legal status. She would have to move back to Mexico to apply for legal status. Then, she could be banned from returning to the United States for up to 10 years.

Martinez helped found an organization that tries to protect undocumented workers. She credits these employees as a critical part of her restaurant's success.

TIMELINE

1873 Levi Strauss and Jacob Davis receive a patent for work pants with rivets that become known as "jeans."

1876 Alexander Graham Bell patents the telephone.

1883 Joseph Pulitzer buys *New York World*, turning it into the country's most popular newspaper.

1901 Andrew Carnegie sells Carnegie Steel Company to J.P. Morgan for $480 million.

1956 One of Oscar de la Renta's early gown designs is featured on the cover of *Life* magazine.

1971 Andy Grove's company, Intel, launches the world's first microprocessor for computers.

1984 Four Ly brothers open the Sugar Bowl Bakery in San Francisco.

Do Won and Jin Sook Chang open Fashion 21, which later becomes the international chain Forever 21.

1989 Ieoh Ming Pei's crowning design, the Louvre Pyramid in Paris, France, is completed.

1995 Jerry Yang and partner David Filo incorporate Yahoo!

1996 Sergey Brin and Larry Page create the Google search engine in Page's dorm room.

2005 Steve Chen, Jawed Karim, and Chad Hurley come up with the idea for YouTube, an online video-sharing platform.

Arianna Huffington starts the online news website *The Huffington Post*.

2006 Steve Chen and fellow YouTube cofounders sell their company to Google for $1.65 billion.

Elon Musk's Tesla Motors (now Tesla, Inc.) unveils its first electric car, the Tesla Roadster.

Indra Nooyi becomes CEO of PepsiCo, changing the company's direction to highlight healthier options.

2007 Biamba Marie Mutombo Hospital, founded by Dikembe Mutombo, opens in Kinshasa, Democratic Republic of the Congo.

Hamdi Ulukaya sends his first shipment of Chobani Greek yogurt to a grocery store on Long Island.

2009 Jan Koum and Brian Acton create WhatsApp, an instant messaging app.

2011 Ayah Bdeir creates littleBits in her creative makerspace.

Valentina Vitols Bello joins Pipeline Angels to help women and nonbinary entrepreneurs.

2015 Reetu Gupta creates the online platform Cirkled In to match colleges and prospective students.

Mina Yoo invents Heroclip, a portable hook.

Chef Cristina Martinez opens South Philly Barbacoa and becomes an advocate for undocumented workers' rights.

2017 Ika Aliyeva launches Femigrants, an online platform for female immigrants.

GLOSSARY

bugged (BUGGD)—placed a hidden microphone

carabiner (kar-uh-BEE-nuhr)—an oblong metal ring with a spring-hinged side

communist (KAHM-yuh-nist)—describing a political system in which the wealth is divided equally among citizens

entrepreneur (ahn-truh-pruh-NUHR)—one who organizes, manages, and takes on the risks of a business enterprise

hierarchy (HYE-uhr-ar-kee)—things arranged into ranks

microchip (MYE-kroh-chip)—a tiny circuit that processes information in a computer

microprocessor (MYE-kroh-PROSS-ess-uhr)—a tiny computer processor contained in a computer chip

Nazi (NOT-see)—a member of a political party led by Adolf Hitler; the Nazis ruled Germany from 1933 to 1945

oppressed (oh-PRESST)—treated in a cruel or unjust way

persecution (puhr-si-KYU-shuhn)—cruel or unfair treatment, often because of race or religious beliefs

prejudice (PREJ-uh-diss)—unfriendly feelings directed against an individual, group, or race

rivet (RIV-it)—a metal bolt with a head at one end used for connecting two or more pieces of material

silicon (SIL-uh-kuhn)—a chemical element used in making computer chips

undocumented (uhn-DAH-kyuh-muhnt-ed)—lacking documents required for legal immigration or residence

READ MORE

Kahn, Brooke. *Home of the Brave: An American History Book for Kids: 15 Immigrants Who Shaped U.S. History.* Emeryville, CA: Rockridge Press, 2019.

Krasner, Barbara. *Making America Great: Famous Immigrant Entrepreneurs.* New York: Enslow Publishing, 2018.

Wallace, Sandra Neil, and Rich Wallace. *First Generation: 36 Trailblazing Immigrants and Refugees Who Make America Great.* New York: Little, Brown Books for Young Readers, 2018.

INTERNET SITES

Immigration
www.kidsdiscover.com/shop/issues/immigration-for-kids

Immigration Facts for Kids
kids.kiddle.co/Immigration

Meet Young Immigrants
teacher.scholastic.com/activities/immigration/young_immigrants

SOURCE NOTES

Page 20, "Mr. Watson, come here . . ." Leonard C. Bruno, "Mr. Watson, Come Here," Library of Congress, https://www.loc.gov/loc/lcib/9904/bell.html, Accessed July 15, 2020.

Page 26, ". . . immigrants and immigration . . ." Mike Sager, "Andy Grove: What I've Learned," *Esquire*, January 29, 2007, https://www.esquire.com/entertainment/interviews/a1449/learned-andy-grove-0500/, Accessed July 15, 2020.

Page 54, "We came here . . ." Llana DeBare, "Sugar Bowl Bakery is a Family Affair," *SFGate*, July 6, 2008, https://www.sfgate.com/business/article/Sugar-Bowl-Bakery-is-a-family-affair-3205820.php, Accessed July 15, 2020.

Page 56, "America has always . . ." Danielle Wiener-Bronner and Cristina Alesci, "Chobani CEO Finds Trump's Travel Ban 'Personal for Me,'" *CNN Money*, January 30, 2017, https://money.cnn.com/2017/01/30/news/chobani-response-travel-ban/, Accessed July 15, 2020.

INDEX